Happy

Easter!

Blessings!

GRADY NUTT

Broadman Press
Nashville, Tennessee

4253-27
ISBN: 0-8054-5327-X

Dewey Decimal Classification: 155.6
Subject Heading: ADULTS

Library of Congress Catalog Card Number: 77-71722
Printed in the United States of America

To Eleanor . . .
   lovely and lovable
   teammate and partner
   joy and comfort
   wife and friend

Introduction

This might well be called the *overture* to *Agaperos* instead of the introduction. An overture tries to blend several themes and related melodies into an appetizer for the main event to follow. In short, it gives me a chance to tell you what the book is about, to thank "those who made it all possible," and to thank you for getting ready to read it.

In that order, then, let me introduce you to *Agaperos*. This book is a collection of several articles I wrote for *The Student*, a magazine published by the National Student Ministries Department of The Sunday School Board, the publishing agency of the Southern Baptist Convention. The magazine is written to college students and tries to address itself to the dilemmas and delights of the college experience. Each issue of the magazine has a theme; I was asked by Norman Bowman and Denise Jones, editor and able associate (respectfully and respectively), to interpret the theme of the issue each month. I would have a theme like hope, love, dreaming, marriage, and so forth, to interpret. It was fun and frustration mixed sweet and sour in my life.

I hit on the technique of inventing a new word almost every month. In interpreting the idea of the essential place of humor in life, I chose to play with the word *humortality*, the obvious linking of *humor* and *mortality*. The dedication of this book to my wife, Eleanor, gives you the clue to my title for the book, *Agaperos*. *Agape* is the Greek word for God's kind of love for us; *eros* is the Greek word for sexually satisfying love. What a neat word for God's kind of love between a man and a woman! We have enjoyed working at that for over twenty years.

Next, let me thank some folks who "made it all possible." Norman Bowman and Denise Jones are two of my closest and dearest friends. For ten years they have given me so much freedom to write and say what I think and feel that I will always owe any success or fulfillment I might find in writing to their faith in me.

I also wish to thank my many close friends who appear by name in these pages. Their friendship and faith have been indispensable commodities in my life; I love and thank them all.

Finally, I thank you for getting ready to read it all. You will find an occasional chuckle, a periodic lump in your throat, and most of the other real emotions. The book is about life, hence about life's emotions.

I would ask you only one favor: Notice that nothing in the book is from the realm of fantasy; it is all from the folks and moments and joys and heavy memories of life at my fingertips. As a favor to yourself, try noticing life's lessons lying at your door like manna—ample, daily, sustaining. Jesus of Nazareth did that, and we call his insights *parables*.

Here's wishing you a bookful of joy!

GRADY NUTT

Contents

Thanksliving

There I sat—
    6:30 A.M.
    on a jet
    unprepared for insight
      like a crusty plot
      before the humbling plow
      makes ready for seeding.
There he came—
    insight on the move
    witty plowpoint
    behind a strong-necked ox—
      crust splitter
      seed driller.
I smiled just looking at him.

To grow an afro like his you'd need
    hairstretchers
    a vacuum
    long arms
        and
    good balance

To find shoes like his you'd need
    a catalog
    patience
    proximity to a weird district
         or
    a father named Flagg!
He definitely took the prize
    first place
    in
    Full-Fro-Slick-Shoe
    competition.

"That seat taken?"
    He pointed to the window seat
    two over from me.
"Help yourself."
    He climbed over.
"My first flight!"

I fly a lot
    and have
    for ten years.
I've noticed that
    most first-timers
    tell you with tight knuckles . . .
        not with words.
He was excited enough
    to make my ten thousandth
    seem like my first
    takeoff all over again.

I had my camera along
    with an arsenal
    of accessories . . .

decided to shoot
some shots of him
on his first flight
get his address
and send them to him.
"You a photographer?"
"No, just a hobby."
Okay with him
to shoot some . . .
shot five . . .
got his address
talked some more . . .
high school senior
on spring vacation
wants to be a psychiatrist
"help people's minds . . ."

My next question brought one of life's great answers:
"You have any hobbies?"
"Just doin' it."
"What do you mean?"
"You know . . .
just bein'."
Just being . . .
his hobby!

Thank you, Wesley Alexander!
Thank you, God!
JUST BEING
I haven't had such a sneaky blessing
in a long,
long time.
A blessing that spoke to me
of a special attitude:
THANKSGIVINGTHANKSLIVINGTHANKS!!

THANKSGIVINGTHANKSLIVINGTHANKS!!
an attitude
that finds treasure
in the plowed field
of routine . . .
that sees daily bread
as a provision
of the Bread of life . . .
that holds a cup
to the water of life
and drinks the mystery of being
with zest.

THANKSGIVINGTHANKSLIVINGTHANKS!!
an eye for perspective
for color
for harmony
for balance . . .
that sees how
"all things
work together for good
to them who love God . . ."
who find in life
that God
loves them.

THANKSGIVINGTHANKSLIVINGTHANKS!!
an ear for the cry of pain
the laugh of joy . . .
the dirge of woe
the lyric of delight . . .
the hollow echo of lonely
the vibes of together . . .
the whisper of help
the shout of love.

14

THANKSGIVINGTHANKSLIVINGTHANKS!!
a touch for appropriate
for right
for compassion
for care
for *sympatico*
for grief
for anger
for *all*
meaningful
deep
feeling.

THANKSGIVINGTHANKSLIVINGTHANKS!!
seeing
hearing
feeling the "God-with-us"
in simple truth
in complexity:
an umbrella in rain/a convertible in sun
wool for a sheep in winter/shears in spring
salt on meat/sugar in tea
coping/hoping

THANKSGIVINGTHANKSLIVINGTHANKS!!
seeing that the beauty of life
is in its pace
direction
movement
ebb/flow . . .
falling in line with its current . . .
conquering in adversity . . .
rejoicing in joyful splendor.

THANKSGIVINGTHANKSLIVINGTHANKS!!
    to live and give ...
    to "do it ..."
    to make a "hobby of being ..."

THANKSWESLEYALEXANDER ...

Celebration

His name is Toby ...
     my twelve-year-old son
     who can get happier
        all over
           about seemingly minor things
     than anyone else I know.

Birthday morning ...
     the other family members
        Eleanor
        Perry
        and I
     stalk into Toby's room
     in wrinkled robes
       bare feet and
       a daze
     to welcome him
     to twelve.

We come like three not-so-wise men
     bearing gifts
     wrapped in Sunday funnies

                    waxed paper and
                    grocery sacks.
Perry . . .
          a bat and a giant Nerf ball.
Eleanor . . .
          a pair of Adidas (super sports shoes)
          size six
          fingers crossed
                    because Toby
                    wears fives.

Grady . . .
          a small Instamatic Kodak.

Perry's first—
          jubilation!
          I got tears in my eyes
          over his unbridled happy!
                    Hugged Perry!
                    Thought to myself:
                    "By suppertime
                    he will have threatened
                    to hit Perry with the bat
                    because he keeps hogging
                    the giant Nerf ball!"
Mine second—
          a yell!
          The dog (Baron)
          began to run and bark.
          "A camera! Wow!"
                    More superlatives . . .
                    More hugs . . .
Eleanor's last—
          a spasm of ecstasy!
          "ADIDAS!! ALRIGHT!!"
                    the ancient ritual
                    of a boy's foot
                    being large enough
                    for a man's shoe.

"They fit!! ALRIGHT!!"
Hadn't even tried them on yet . . .
immaterial.
(Whistlelikeforlostdog!)
Emotional backflips
while cross-legged
on the bed.
Joy!
Celebration!

I watched him walk/run/leap/dart/dash
to school
in his
ADIDAS!! ALRIGHT!!
and teared
a bit more.
Because
I remembered hearing him say
only three weeks before
how much joy it brought him
to be able to give gifts
to people he loved.

That was the dark side of his moon
now full harvest
that gave his capacity
to receive gifts
such depth.

To celebrate life is to know
how to receive life's good gifts
because we know how to give them.

Somewhere I read:
"Hold on to your life and lose it;
give it away and hold on to it!"

ADIDAS!! ALRIGHT!!
Celebration!

CELEBRATE!

Superword.
Full of promise
      hope
      wonder
      emotion
      vigor
      pleasure
      good memory
      fury
      action . . .

CELEBRATE!

Grasping with gusto
      the ring
      on life's merry-go-round
      and knowing unquestionably
            you
            are
            a
            winner.

CELEBRATE!

When life presses your mind into a December
      feeling the warm rays
      of May
      because you have coped/hoped
      your way through.

CELEBRATE!

Attempt new things
    face new directions
    meet new friends
    open new doors
    have new experiences
    know new joys.

CELEBRATE!

Say to the surging sea
    "I can float!"
  to the bucking maverick
    "I can ride!"
  to the craggy peak
    "I can climb!"
  to the difficult melody
    "I can sing!"

CELEBRATE!

Swing your pick
    and find a diamond;
Plant an acorn
    and climb your oak.

CELEBRATE!

Know this is the day the Lord has made
    and
    it is very good.

ADIDAS!! ALRIGHT!!

Glassdarklyfacetoface

There I was—
    Highway 31
    north to Kokomo
    above Indianapolis—
        moving at a radar-defying pace
        (no brag, just fact)
        late for an engagement.
There it was—
    guarding an intersection
    for its seventieth year
        erect as a Buckingham sentry
        on a Queen-coming-by-day.
Even at that speed
    my noticer was noticing
    noticeably well
        and I noticed . . .
            the sign out front
            two feet by four feet
            adorned by a formal mouse.

The composite view
    jerked me from above-radar
    to notice-pace
        and I whipped around
        in a noninterstate four-lane
        and went by
        once again.
I was right!
    A Methodist church building
    with a commercial sign out front . . .
        formal mouse
        sporting cane
            top hat
            tux
            spats
    and the new name of a noble old edifice:
        "THE CHURCH MOUSE."
Snatched ever-ready camera
        filters
        tripod
        note pad
        film
    and went snap-crazy for ten minutes
    to the bewilderment of the owner
    and three customers.
Dashed in to secure the story . . .
    this is what I found.
 1902—the crucial year—
    a hearty band
    of dedicated
      affluent
      Methodists
    decided to build here
    on the present intersection
    a monumental house of worship.

They did—
    down to the loveliest windows—
        stained-glass
        French imports
        hand rolled
        now worth fifty cents per square inch!—
    I've ever seen in any church.
Rural cathedral—
    scene of funeral
        wedding
        confirmation
        decision
        fellowship
        conflict
        worship
    for almost three fourths of a century.
Times changed—
    young Methodists
    moved on to Kokomo
            Indianapolis
    and such places . . .
        church struggled to exist . . .
        finally folded
        and went "out of business,"
        merging into larger congregations nearby.
Two years boarded up—
    then bought by
    Mrs. R. K. Dwyer and son
    of Kokomo
        and turned into a
        gift shop
        greeting card/antique/waxed owl
            outlet.

Surely the original idea-haver
    in this Methodist outpost
    must have whirled in his grave
    when Mrs. Dwyer and son
    signed the deed
    that made the
        church house
      "THE CHURCH MOUSE!"
But how often it happens:
    great aspirations
    lofty dreams
    high ambitions
        fade
        die
        "go out of business"
    when new visionaries
    move to Kokomo
    and board up the windows
    of yesterday's resolve.
Many a youth has hit college
    fresh out of such
    deep intention
        only to begin right away
        to turn the rich heritage
        of his spiritual growth
        into a wax-owl roost!
Your task:
    to enrich the best of such dreams
    to transform inadequate visions
    to unfetter Godly hope
    to unboard windows
    to shape tomorrow's vessel
        from yesterday's clay.
Paul, apostle, said that
    we see through a glass darkly (today)
    but then (tomorrow) face to face.

Always has been . . .
Always will be . . .
 the church is in transit
  is becoming
  is pregnant with change
 when it is dreamed and hoped
 with courage and commitment.
And it is your task . . .
 to live in the glassdarklyfacetoface
 uncertainty of the church's *next*
 with dreams of courage and determination.
Church house;
CHURCHMOUSE;
Glassdarklyfacetoface . . .

GLASSDARKLYFACETOFACE . . .
 dashing in a relay of destiny
 eyes forward
 hand back
  to receive the baton
  carried by forebears
   saints
   believers
   Christ himself
  certain that the "gates of hell"
  will fold like a cardboard bomb shelter
  before such dedication.
GLASSDARKLYFACETOFACE . . .
 not seeing far away
 but seeing for a way . . .
  not understanding all
  but understanding enough . . .
   not grasping
   but reaching . . .

GLASSDARKLYFACETOFACE . . .
  a high hope
  stamped *visionimpossible*
      lived
      planned
      held with commitment
      till harvest comes
      and the barn is full.
GLASSDARKLYFACETOFACE . . .
  knowing the parable is true
  that "what we sow
        we reap"
  and learning further
    "what we *wish* to reap
    we *must* sow . . ."
GLASSDARKLYFACETOFACE . . .
  learning that maybe the glass is dark
  because it is full of stained saints holding lambs
      and angels flying
      in brilliant blues
          greens
          reds
          yellows . . .
  and that you can love your windows
  more than you love God . . .
      you can love having your way
      more than you can love walking his way . . .
GLASSDARKLYFACETOFACE . . .
  learning that children
  are as hard to raise
  as corn
    wheat
    or beans

and that some folks
try to raise children
like corn
   wheat
   or beans . . .
GLASSDARKLYFACETOFACE . . .
   discovering as you mature
   that what you get at forty
   is seldom what you planned
         dreamed at twenty-two.
GLASSDARKLYFACETOFACE . . .
   as a longtime follower of Christ
   and devotee to his church
         that there is the live option
         that the next generation
         may sell wax owls
         where you knelt for communion . . .
GLASSDARKLYFACETOFACE . . .
   they can buy your church
   but they can never
         purchase
               your
                  dreams . . .

Agaperos

Old Greek teachers were smiling . . .
    winking at each other . . .
    elbowing gently . . .
        G. Nutt had been brainwashed
        (for the right reasons, though)
        and was thinking their way.

The word was out in Greek circles
    that I was interpreting
    (in poetry-designed-to-throat-lump)
        the concept of *love*.)

Wads of disappointing beginnings
    lay piled around my typewriter . . .
    reading great *love*-interpreters
    (*other* great *love*-interpreters,
    I add, humbly)
        left my soul desert-dry:
            they had not said it all
            but
            I could not think up
            what was missing!

When the world is waiting for you
　　　and you can't come through
　　　you ache for said world.

Then, looking at a rain puddle
　　　on a flat roof outside the window
　　　gears shifted
　　　　　ideas meshed
　　　　　　　and I blew old Greeks
　　　　　　　　　old Greek minds . . .

I was an *agape*-captive.

Years of seminars
　　　seminary
　　　lectures
　　　magazine articles
　　　　　had done it . . .
　　　　　　　maybe not maliciously
　　　　　but
　　　　　had done it all the same.

They had me hearing *love*
　　　and thinking
　　　　　automatically
　　　　　instinctively
　agape—
　　　　　undeserved love
　　　　　God's kind of love
　　　　　love that seeks no reward
　　　　　love that takes the initiative—
　　　and not thinking
　　　unless with guilt

eros—
>passion
>supreme man/woman thing
>physical
>sex.

I stamped my foot (on the typewriter)
>threw down another wad of first effort
>wound in another clean sheet
>and prepared to type errors
>in defense of eros—
>>also
>>a Greek word . . .

It was church-related "sexperts"
>who first made me feel guilty
>about some very normal stuff
>in the boy/girl
>>male/female category . . .
>ideas like
>>no kissing till marriage
>>no hand-holding in prayer gardens.

My memory and feelings are the testifiers here . . .
>not a manuscript
>or tape recording . . .
>>my gut-memory is
>>>for Christians
>>>eros is enemy
>>>agape is Savior.

People of all ages used my type as the example
>of what courtship
>should be for the Christian:
>>mixed leaf-raking
>>group marshmallow toasts
>>prayer dates.

On the surface I took their advice . . .
  underneath I was a smoldering cauldron
    scheming
    fantasizing
    conjuring . . .
      and marriage was almost catastrophe.

I grinned at me in college
  when I dated
  I was the campus example-in-residence
  of Christian on a date . . .
    not entirely because of my
    sterling character
      largely because
      I didn't have a car
      until three months
      before my wedding!
  the picture of *agape.*

I grinned at me in marriage . . .
  1 Corinthians 13 at the bedside
  prayer
  confession of mutual unworthiness
    and then the pent-up release
    of years of
    WAITTILLMARRIAGE
    that had my new bride
    terrified that anytime now
    he's coming home from the church office!
  Captain Eros!

I grin at all of this in the full moon
  of my fifteenth wedding anniversary . . .
  fifteen years that have taught me
    one supremely valuable lesson:

agape and *eros*
are both good words
  and make one super word
together:
  AGAPEROS.

Therefore, to my dear wife, Eleanor,
  I doff the husband-hat
    blush at my "know-it-all"
    commend her willingness to grow
    to put up with me
    to make love work.

I remind myself that it is not uncommon
  to "love thy neighbor"
  and forget the joy
  of "loving thy wife."

I thank her for the
  "everything-she-always-wanted-to-know"
  and got courage to ask.

I smile at her deep love for me
  that overlooks
  Grand Canyon ignorance
    and notices
    mustard seeds of
      "he finally . . ."

I hold her close on a chilly night
  grateful for her
  fantastic figure
    love for good clothes
      growing awareness that she is beautiful . . .
        thinks of us
        and not
        him and me.

Agaperos—
　　loving right
　　for the right reasons
　　with the right person.
AGAPEROS . . .

AGAPEROS
　　Learning that *making out*
　　is not always making it . . .
　　　　finding that you may be able
　　　　to love together
　　　　but may not be able
　　　　　　to live together . . .

AGAPEROS
　　Abiding in deep affection
　　after the new has worn off . . .
　　　　tackling marriage-killing problems
　　　　and making them—
　　　　　　years later—
　　　　　　the stuff *together*
　　　　　　is made of . . .

AGAPEROS
　　Joyfully "becoming one flesh"
　　in the healthy knowledge that
　　　　"male and female created
　　　　he them . . ."
　　　　　　that it was all God's idea
　　　　　　and that he thought of all
　　　　　　his ideas as
　　　　　　very good . . .
　　　　　　　　and this one
　　　　　　　　was very, very good . . .

AGAPEROS
Discovering that *agape* . . .
selfless
God's kind of
unmerited
initiative-taking
love . . .
understanding *eros* . . .
physical
passion
male/female
sex . . .
best of all . . .

AGAPEROS
Finding the absolute paganism
in the frequently used candle service
in many current weddings . . .
three candles on a stand
two on the outside burning
one in center unlit;
"I now pronounce you . . ."
and the new couple
takes a burning candle
each
and together light
the center candle
and then
each
blows his/her candle out!
Agaperos knows
you don't have
to blow your candle out
to create something unique
beautiful
enduring
together . . .

AGAPEROS
> Loving each other
> with everything you have
> to give
>> share
>> enjoy
>>> together...

AGAPEROS
> Knowing God's kind of love
> isn't just Greek...
>> can be known
>> by *agape*-captives
>> by *eros*-slaves...
>>> and will set you free...
>>> indeed!

AGAPEROS
> *Hurray!*

Soarunafraid

Dennis the Menace lives
  next door to
  Mr. Wilson . . .
    crotchety old crank
    the kind
    whose windows
    softballs love to find . . .

I used to live
  next door to
  Mr. Larsen . . .
    kid lover
    the kind
    kids love to find . . .

I found him often.

Not only did he know kids . . .
  He also knew kites . . .
  He *really* knew kites . . .

box kites
dime store kites
homemade kites . . .
    he really, *really* knew
    homemade kites
    he home made . . .

One stands out in my mind
  because it took a group
to fly it
  and always struck fear
  into the local
  Air Force base . . .
    they were scrambled
    to check it out
    twice in one week.

What a kite!
  The crosspieces of wood
  were bamboo fishing poles . . .
    the paper was
    butcher paper . . .
      the twine was
      the kind you could tie
      a moose to a tree with
      while you went for help.

Mr. Larsen drove a city bus
  and got home at a decent hour
  every afternoon . . .
    in windy weather
    we beat a path
    to the great kite flyer
    and he'd join us
    on a vacant lot
    often.

The big kite—
  Air Force frightener—
    could only be flown
    on windy
    all-day-Saturdays.

It took a group
  to unwind the moosebind
  hold the seven-foot cloud-eater
  upright
  and get it started.

Even the group couldn't hold it . . .
  we anchored it
  to a winch
  on the bumper of
  Mr. Larsen's pickup . . .
    my memory tells me
    we sent out a half-mile
    of cord on that thing . . .
      did it
      ever fly!

It was natural I should try
  to build a bumper-bender
  of my own . . .
    mine hardly
    rattled a
    canary cage!

It looked great on my garage floor
  and that is as high
  as it flew
    till kitemaster Larsen
    helped me send it
    up right.

I remember now so clearly
   standing on the lot
   with my kite twirling
   like a baton
      with fire
      on each end
      at Orange Bowl
      half time.

About three of those twirls
   and then it would nose
   into the ground . . .
      Charlie Brown
      could fly kites
      out there . . .
         no trees.

Mr. Larsen pushed his bus cap
   back on his head
   and set his lunch pail down
   and walked to me . . .
      I was untying
      some bedsheet tail
      so it would really get up there.

Patiently he showed me a valuable lesson . . .
   more tail
      not *less* tail
   was the answer . . .
      three or four
      more strips
      and it almost
      got the Air Force
      up for the third time
      that week!

From the seven-footer on a moose leash
   to my three-footer on sewing thread
   I learned
   these two lessons
   for men who soar
      free and high
      in the midst of life:

One . . .
   I wanted to see the winch
   break and set the seven-footer
   loose so it could really go
   high . . .
      I learned
         the tension on the cord
         created resistance
         which enabled it
         to fly.

Two . . .
   I wanted to take weight
   off my three-footer
   so it could rise . . .
      I learned
         the weight of the tail
         stabilized the windcraft
         and enabled it
         to rise.

From these lessons, a lesson:
   we soar highest
   when solidly anchored;
      life's weighty burden
      stabilizes for real growth.

Real freedom is not
  unfettered do-as-you-please
  unabashed self-tending
  ruleless abandon ...
    self-pleasing
    for self's sake
    alone will put you
      in the clods
      not in the clouds!

Life is emptiest for the person
  who thinks
  a succession of highs
  totals a *real* ...
    fullest for him
    who discovers
    burdens and boundaries
    help you rise
    above clods *and* clouds ...

SOARUNAFRAID ...

SOARUNAFRAID ...
  Bite the wind
    gnaw it like
    Lazarus would ravish
    a prime rib ...
  know it is your friend
    your support
    your strength ...

SOARUNAFRAID ...
  Know ecstasy is *not*
    giddy temporal pleasure
    star-spangled sensuality
    imposed highs ...

but . . .
    disciplined hope
    in the midst of struggle
    that says assuredly . . .
        no matter
        the odds . . .
    "This, too, shall pass!"

SOARUNAFRAID . . .
    Pull with all your strength
    at your "moosebinder"
        knowing it will lift you up
        not drag you down . . .

SOARUNAFRAID . . .
    Bear the world's slavery
    with unbeatable vigor
        then give the world
        a spiritual that will
        blister clapping hands
            and stamping feet
            with its joyous
            rhythm . . .

SOARUNAFRAID . . .
    Run hard/run fast
    let the blast of your own
    "jet stream"
        dry the sweat
        on your brow
        and discover
            too soon the race is over
            too late we realize
                the real joy
                was in the running . . .

SOARUNAFRAID . . .
  Find what apostles
  rubbed elbows with . . .
      God in human flesh
      Jesus of Nazareth . . .
          in whom God
          stooped lowest
          and
          rose highest . . .

SOARUNAFRAID . . .
  Let Paul, apostle of note,
  teach you:
      "We have this *confidence*
      in Christ Jesus . . ."
  clods never look the same
  to a man who
      has seen the top
      of the clouds . . .

SOARUNAFRAID . . .

Hopealongcasually

Wayne Oates
   my friend
      teacher
      and
      colleague
   for the past decade-plus
   has a son
         Charlie
   now college age.

When Charlie was about ten
   he was busy at play
   in the den of their home
      preparing to fly
      a balsa airplane . . .
         rubber-band-driven
         39¢ each
         bought with allowance
         pride-and-joy of the day.

He began piecing it all together—
    wings through the long center slot
    tail assembly
      sideways and
      upright
        right . . .
           wheels on wire brace . . .
    and *two* rubber bands!

Charlie got it just so-so in his hands
  and began winding
  the rubber bands
  to the maximum power.

Smoothly it wound at first—
  then winding slowed
  to a crawl—
    you could feel the power
    yearning to unleash itself—
      the rubber bands formed
      into weird curlicues
      and knots up and down
      the plane's spine . . .
    the plane trembled
    like a receiver
    on the kickoff.

Then Charlie aimed the balsa missile
  down a clear path
  lengthways in the den—
    lay on the den floor
    to watch his week's allowance
    bring him an unwinding
      moment
      of joy . . .
      freed it like a white dove
      at the Olympics . . .

Away it flew!
   right down the den
   over parents' heads
         ducking behind
         being-read newspapers
         over a lampshade
   past his brother Bill's ear
         into
         a
         solid wall!

A pile of splinters . . .
   a seventeen-piece propeller . . .
         one wheel present/one unaccounted for . . .
            two panting rubber bands . . .
               and a ten-year-old
               with a tear
               ready to roll
                     rummaging
                     through
                     the ruins.

Dr. Oates, Mother Oates, and Bill
   came up from behind
   Courier-Journals
      and sofa arms
      like Londoners
         after an
         air raid
         ALL CLEAR!

No one spoke . . .
   no one needed to . . .
      that kind of misery
      hates company.

Quiet resumed for five minutes
   then Charlie got up
   and started out of the room
      twirling the rubber bands
      on his fintertips
      and . . .
         WHISTLING!

The other Oates looked at each other . . .
   the father—
         who only knows best
         when he knows what's up—
   stopped Charlie.

"Hey, Guy . . .what's up?
   A moment ago
   tears in the rubble . . .
      now a whistle
      and a snap in your step . . ."

And Charlie explained . . .
   with a twinkle in his eye . . .
   moist but twinkling . . .

"I just decided
   I'm going to take
   these rubber bands
   and make me a slingshot!"

They all laughed
   and prepared to duck
   rocks
   instead of balsa!

And such is the stuff hope is made of—
 making monuments out of rubble
 whistling your way to renewal
 bouncing off walls
  but bouncing up!

Hope . . .
 the trademark of confidence
 the fuel of achievement . . .

HOPEALONGCASUALLY!

HOPEALONGCASUALLY

Two-lane hilly winding highway . . .
 trucks
 senior-citizen slowpokes
 tractor pulling hayrake
  mile after two-lane
   hilly
   winding mile . . .
 temper boiling
 theological adjectives
 neck craning
 brake lights burning out—
  then it appears:
   a sign on the right
   "Four-lane highway
   three miles ahead"
  you relax
  you cool down
  your neck uncranes
  you whistle . . .
  you move in solid hope
   not wishing for relief
   any longer
   but confident it is there!

you've a reason for easin'—
    you *saw the sign!*

HOPEALONGCASUALLY

"And the word of God
    became a human being
    and walked among
    US!"
        God's great
        "4 lane; 3 miles"
        sign:
            so we *hope*
            not *wish!*

HOPEALONGCASUALLY

Seeing visions
Dreaming dreams
Fostering great ambitions
Winding up for soaring flight
Smacking into solid walls
Searching through ruins
    for a residue of power
Whistling at last
    with new resolve . . .

HOPEALONGCASUALLY

Facing Good Friday
    without being aware
    of Easter;
but facing Good Friday
    never doubting
    Easter . . .

HOPEALONGCASUALLY

Taking a semester final
  with the good feeling
  that you studied
    remembered
    and
    can relate it
    all ...

HOPEALONGCASUALLY

Getting a bill
  you can pay
  because you saved ...

HOPEALONGCASUALLY

In short, confidence ...

HOPEALONGCASUALLY

Agreeing with Paul
  that faith, hope, and love
  abide ...
  that love is the greatest ...
  that hope makes it possible ...

HOPEALONGCASUALLY

Peace ...

Calibrate/ Graduate/ Celebrate

Frank Hart "Pogo" Smith has been
   one of my special friends
   for twenty years.

He should spell it Frank "Heart" Smith . . .
   if you know him, you agree . . .
   if you don't agree, you don't know him!

Recently my family spent a couple of days
   with his family
   and enjoyed being
   in their home.

The decor is "them" . . .
   not early American
   but cast-off American . . .
     not antique
     but "garage sale"!

Pogo works . . .
   loves his family
   serves mankind with zest
   participates in church
      and
      attends
      garage sales.

There have been many phenomena
   in the world
   without explanation:
      the Loch Ness monster
      the abominable snowman
      swamp gas
      and the Nashville
         Saturday A.M.
         lightning-fast
         street-level
         blue flash . . .

The Nashville flash was solved
   in August '72—
      it was found to be
      Pogo
      bound
      for a garage sale!

Pogo frequently meets a man at these sales
   who is a collector
   of antique clocks . . .
      clocks are his thing.

He tinkers with his clocks
   all the.time . . .

they tick
   bong
   tock
   and chime
from footlockers
   mantels
   dressers
   hallways
   and attics.

A man obsessed with old clocks!

But ... you expected this! ... an interesting fact:
  this man
  is never on time
  for anything!

I sat at Pogo's big maple table
  and laughed with him
  about this "dumb-clock" ...
    somewhat typical
    of so many people
    who understand the *mechanics*
    but rarely the *essence* of life!

And now I think of the mortarboard martyrs ...
  marching with tassels
  in tired faces
    collecting degrees
    like "dumb-clock" collects
      Seth Thomas mantel bongers ...
  experts on facts
  short on insight;
    experts on ideas
    short on experience.

Fully normal.
Young adulthood is the gristmill
   for the grain
of adolescence . . .
      what you've been taught
      you now must learn
         what you've dreamed
         you must now attempt.

The word *commencement* has undergone cultural shock:
   it started out
   to mean begin
      start
      initiate
   and has come to mean finish
            get-over-with
            be pronounced adequate.

Commencement does mean to begin
            to set out
            to launch
            to be fully qualified
               to try
               to succeed
               to fail.

Ever get asked:
   "What are you going to be?"
Ever answer with a shrug?

I never heard that question answered:
   "An adult."
That is the hardest thing to be
   of all . . .
            and will take all your years
               all your energy.

Step on in . . .
     the water's fine . . .
  and remember the words
  of Walt Kelly,
     the cartoonist
     who thought up
     Pogo (the possum):
          "Too soon we breast the tape
          and too late we realize
          the real joy lay in the running!"

The Carpenters ought to sing at every graduation:
  "We've Only Just Begun . . ."

Welcome . . .
  and congratulations . . .

You've learned to *calibrate* . . .
     to measure time and eternity
     for depth and meaning . . .

You've prepared to *graduate* . . .
     to begin with zeal
     the process of maturing . . .

You're ready to *celebrate* . . .
     not to prime happiness
     but to let it flow!!!

CALIBRATE/GRADUATE/CELEBRATE!!!

CALIBRATE/GRADUATE/CELEBRATE!!!
  Let the trappings around you
  Be you . . .
     Find meaning your way
     in the things that fulfill.

CALIBRATE/GRADUATE/CELEBRATE!!!
  Wrestle with *essence*
        as well as
        with *mechanics* ...
        unravel the Greek concepts
        of *chronos*—
            chronological
            diary
            "where-you-went-what-you-did"
                time—
        and *kairos*—
            "what-all-that-meant"
                time—

CALIBRATE/GRADUATE/CELEBRATE!!!
  Be more concerned
      with the joy of running
      than with the necessity
          of arriving ...
Know you must find meaning
    in transit ...
        for you may be
        struck down
        in mid-method!

CALIBRATE/GRADUATE/CELEBRATE!!!
  Take heart when you aren't sure
      at twenty-three what you want to do
      at sixty
        that Jesus was thirty
        when he finally said
            "This one thing
            I do!"

CALIBRATE/GRADUATE/CELEBRATE!!!
Find relief in the fact
  that it is harder
  to be "an adult"
  than to be
    "an accountant"!

CALIBRATE/GRADUATE/CELEBRATE!!!
Know the peace that comes
  when you use facts
  instead of
  being used by facts!

CALIBRATE/GRADUATE/CELEBRATE!!!
Let the future be a joy
  and not a burden ...
Know the past is a foundation
  and not an anchor ...
Hold the present in steady hands
  like ordinary clay
  about to become
  a collector's item!
And ...
  Go with God!!

Souljourn

I've probably heard an above-average
   share
   of missionary
   testimony
     folklore
       and legend.

I've seen enough slides of Africa
   to have my citizenship
   transferred to Nigeria
   without leaving
   Louisville!

Many move me; a few bore me.

This one moves me . . .

A native in Africa became a Christian
   and after some time
   declared that God
   had impressed upon him

the need to give his life
as a minister
to his own people.

The remarkable change in his life
caused all who knew him
to cheer . . .
what good news that
this good man
should give his life
to preach the good news.

Some time was spent
by the mission leaders
preparing this remarkable young man
for his task.

Then came the great day—
he was ordained
to the Christian ministry.

The village was out in force . . .
The mission was aglow with hope . . .
The candidate was eager to go . . .

Words were said—
hands cupped over his head . . .
prayers were offered . . .
a Bible was presented . . .
and a gift
was given—
a new bicycle!

The mission had gathered—
  all possible funds
  were pooled
  so that the new preacher
  could get about the country
  to preach the gospel.

Tears flowed on all faces—
  glistening like chocolate
  icing in the rain!

At last the newly ordained minister
  stood to face
  his friends
  and encouragers.

"I thank you all from the depths of my heart!
  Your love and support
  mean more to me
  than you can know.

"However, I cannot accept
  the beautiful bicycle
  you have given me today.
    (Moist eyes widened . . .)
  There is a good reason.
    (Eyebrows arched . . .)

"God has called me to minister to my people . . .
  I fear that if I were
  to *pedal* about
  rather than *walk*
    I might hasten past
    opportunities to share
    with people who need me . . ."
And in that spirit continued . . .

That mission epic reminds me
  of two other items of interest:
    (1) The movie title:
        "IF THIS IS TUESDAY
        THIS MUST BE BELGIUM."
  and
    (2) The man who returned from
        New York with a sackful of
        stubs from Broadway shows;
        he had collected stubs at each
        theater but had not seen a
        single performance!

We tend in life to
  waltz past the crucial
  collect souvenirs more
    than encounter experience
  and move numbly
    through chances to learn.

Like a man leaping out of his car
  to snapshoot Hoover Dam
  and race on
    we glance at
    what should be pondered
    and forge ahead, saying:
      "Well, I've seen that."

Better to spend time in Belgium
than keep schedule through it;
  better to walk in awareness
  than pedal past need;
    better to see one play
    than have a sack of stubs;

better to see Disney World
than buy slides;
    better to drive with a friend
    than Grand Marshal the Rose Parade;
better to see
than look;
    better to listen
    than hear.

And I remember a parable—
    of professional ministers
    "pedaling" to the temple
    past a ditch-dweller
    bleeding for their concern—
        and of a traveling salesman
        from a hostile country
        who "walked" slow enough
        to notice
            and "donkeyed" him
            to help.

We get to a lot of territory
    we never see!
We see a lot that doesn't matter
    and count it
    as heirloom.

To travel in awareness—
    to SOULJOURN—
    to be sensitive to life
    to living
    to people
    to self.

SOULJOURN!
"Pussycat, pussycat,
where have you been?"
    "I've been to London
    to see the Queen!"
"Pussycat, pussycat,
What did you there?"
    "I spied a little mouse
    under her chair!"
Oh, Pussycat!
    How typical!
    You missed the Queen
        in the chair
    staring at the mouse
        under it!

SOULJOURN!
To absorb,
not just to *observe*
    as you move
    through life . . .
to lower your bucket deep
into the well and wealth of life
    and drink it dry
    rather than sip and run.

SOULJOURN!
The exciting knowledge
that the world is a neighborhood
    not a supermarket
    for travel agents!

SOULJOURN!
Meaning and memories in the heart—
not just souvenirs
    on the
    mantel!

SOULJOURN!
Knowing who you are
    where you are
    who your brothers are
    where your brothers are!
Feeling the pain
    the pathos
    the joy
    the calm of life!
Doing all you can
    when you can
    where you find need!

SOULJOURN!
and Godspeed!

Crocus/Hocus/Pocus

The sun got on my neighborhood
    and warmed March
    a month early this spring
    and said:
       "Here, crocus!"
    and clods flew like popcorn
      with the lid off . . .

The annual flower-fling was on!

The crocus
  hyacinths
  jonquils
  and tulips raced to be first
    to color the winter-killed yard
    with white
      blue
      pink
      yellow
      red
      lavender
      and joy!

The crocus won . . .
　　can the tulip be far behind?

I think you should read this first in autumn . . .
　　when this year says good-bye
　　to what March said hello
　　to.

The good-bye will be bronze
　　　　　　　　　amber
　　　　　　　　　gold
　　　　　　　　　burgundy
　　　　　　　　　and grand . . .
　　thanks to the *hocus pocus*
　　　of the crocus.

I owe this insight to Elton Trueblood
　　who prayed on a Louisville
　　autumn-colored morning:
　　　"Lord, thank you
　　　for all the
　　　unnecessary colors . . ."

Is a blue flower any more important
　　than a yellow flower?
Is a red leaf more crucial
　　than an orange leaf?

It means that God thinks *beauty*
　　is every bit as important
　　as *function* . . .
　　　not "more important . . ."
　　　but "different than . . ."

No small wonder to me that you see
    the first crocus
    just about
    Easter . . .
        spring's "Oh, yes I can!"
        to winter's "Oh, no you don't!"

Further crocus info . . .
    I never have any in my yard
    and Mr. Yentzch (next door)
    always does.

The difference is that Mr. Yentzch
    plants bulbs in the fall
    while I watch football
    and gripe about leaves to rake.

Life gives crocus-power to
    crocus-planters!

I haven't quoted Hebrews to you yet—
    now's the right time:
        Chapter 12 has a verse 11
        which verily readeth,
           "Naturally,
           all discipline seems
           hard to take
           at the time."

You are in the time of life when
    discipline seems hard to take
    all the time . . .
        and more discipline is required all the time.

Perhaps there's a new semester before you
    like a fresh-washed slate
    ready to be filled
    with energy and insight
      and you'll likely
      be normal
      and fill it
      with doodles . . .

I always wanted *A*'s
    but hated libraries
    had no self-discipline
    had a non-learn yearn.

I wanted October yellow
    without March sweat.

Life has a grindstone for every nose
    a yoke for every neck
    a songbird for every cherry bough
    a crocus for every Yentzch.

You do your thing
    (plant, water, dream, work)
      and the crocus will do his.

Get hold of now and its challenge
    and make this year
    count.

Frankly, the *hocus pocus* of the crocus
    is that
    sweat-watered bulbs
    bloom best!

CROCUS/HOCUS/POCUS

Enduring winter snow with a grin
    knowing the delicate flowers
    are the first up
    to face the uncertainty
    of frost
       late snow
       unseasonal cool
       and preschool pluckers.

CROCUS/HOCUS/POCUS

Hot autumn laps in an unairconditioned gym
    that result
    in a March trophy
    at the state tourney ...

CROCUS/HOCUS/POCUS

Self-determination!
  The self determined to
    hit it
    and
    get it!

CROCUS/HOCUS/POCUS

Good beginnings demand
    good prebeginnings ...
       to get flowers in the warm
       you plant bulbs in the cool.

CROCUS/HOCUS/POCUS

A new friend you just instinctively know
 will get to be
 an old friend . . .
A required course you dread
 that turns out
 to be your major . . .
An idea that fascinates you
 then
 changes your life . . .

CROCUS/HOCUS/POCUS

Borderline cockiness in June
 because
 you've kept all
 your New Year's
 resolutions . . .

CROCUS/HOCUS/POCUS

Learning that the same oven
 that melts wax
 hardens clay . . .
  live knowing
  you get out
  what you put in . . .

CROCUS/HOCUS/POCUS

Sorry about that, tulip . . .
 maybe
 next
 year . . .

Grattitude

Herewith are recorded jewels
  from the vault
  of a thankful man,
    yours truly . . .

Several years ago I saw the movie
  The Yearling . . .
    story of a land-clearing
      hard-working
      low-income
      high-hoped family.

The father impressed upon me
  in my very inflexible
    very literal
    mind-shut
    early religious experience
    something very profound.

Each evening he would rinse hands
   in a basin
   'neath an oak
   near a well
     then come to the
     sparse but hot food
     on a rough-cut table.

He'd place his hat on his chairback
   not bow his head
   not close his eyes
   and not piously pray
   thus:
     "Thanks again
     for the vittles,
     Lord.
     Amen."

I saw the same seriousness caricatured
   by Charlie McDaniel—
     irreverent but reverent
     loud but pensive
     college classmate.

At a "Greasy Spoon" near Baylor U.
   a host of the lower-income
       higher-outgo
   group used to gather
   for lunch.

One day each of us
   received our burgers
   before Charlie did
     and promptly
     and mannerlessly
     attacked them

with voracious vengeance
and flying elbows.

Charlie's burger came.

In the midst of our snarling
   he said most piously—
      more so than we thought possible—
   "Men, I'd like to say grace
      if you could hold it down."

Ashamed.
Awkward.
Embarrassed
  we all dropped
    heads
    burgers
    forks
    French fries
and prepared for Charlie
to say grace.

Others around noticed our devotion
      and our display of it
      and our dedication
        to displaying
        our devotion . . .
  "not ashamed of the gospel"
right out in public!

The quiet grew louder.

Finally, Charlie—like the timing genius he was—
  stood
  cleared his throat
  and shouted:
      "GRACE!"

Uproar!!!

This last jewel comes from my closest friend
   for many, many years—
   Elmore Averyt (of Henrietta, Texas, fame!).

We attended a small school
   with five hundred students
   our freshman year in college.

All the student body
   could eat in the cafeteria
   for each meal.

Each (except for the questionably devoted)
   usually bowed his/her head
   and asked a silent blessing
   on his/her food.

Elmore used to love *most* of all
   to sit at a table
   with the conspicuously holy
   and await a joint head-bow
   from four or five at once
      then quietly announce
      in the midst of silent grace:
      "Last one through's a fanatic!"

Conclusions:

You can bless enchiladas
      tacos
      tamales
      and jalapenos
   and they will *still* give you
   "Montezuma's Revenge!"

You can bless coffee
   and it will *still*
   keep you awake!

You can *fail* to bless steak
   and it will *still*
   taste good!

The blessing does nothing at all to the food!
The blessing does everything for the eater!

You must learn to work for it
   as hard as you pray over it!

The "attitude-of-gratitude"
   helps you see that Paul—
      "apostle of note"—
   was right after all:
      "All things work together
      for good
      to them
      who *really* love God."

The "attitude-of-gratitude" . . .

GRATTITUDE!

GRATTITUDE!

The awareness that food is blessed
         life is blessed
         blessers are blessed
   by God
   and not
   by words.

GRATTITUDE!

God is thanked
  by the way I live
  not by the way I pray!

GRATTITUDE!

Praying over leftovers
  with awareness
  that yesterday
  we had too much!

GRATTITUDE!

Learning the gospel according to
  Karl Menninger—
  psychiatrist
  writer
  people-knower:
    "Our capacity to give
    is one of the best
    indications of
    mental health—
      I have known
      very few
      generous people
      who were
      mentally ill!"

GRATTITUDE!

Learning the gospel according to
  Gene Cotton—
  folk singer
  friend
  giver
  people-lover:

"Come into my house
take my bed
drink my wine
break my bread—
    cause all that I have
    belongs to you ..."

(and it does ...)

GRATTITUDE!

Learning the gospel according to
    Rod Foster—
    seminarian
    gentle Christian
    cancer-victim
    people-helper:
    "When I learned
    that I had cancer
    and did not have
    long to live
        I did *not* pray:
        O, God, *why!*
        I prayed:
        O, God, what now?"

GRATTITUDE!

To yell "Grace!"
    again over vittles (and vitals)
    like a fanatic!!

GRATTITUDE!

Friendcarnation

I failed chemistry in a big way—
  with class
  with distinction—
  Dr. Bill Cook
  (Baylor chemistry prof)
  noted with pride
  that I had done
  the most ingenious job
  of failing chemistry
    he'd ever seen . . .

He submitted three of my test papers
  to *Reader's Digest*—
    they regretted
    they couldn't publish them
    because they were
    overstocked on fiction!

I never got the hang of it.

I never got my grades high enough
  to withdraw
    passing.

Problem was—
  a brilliant dodo-grad student
  was enrolling
  chemistry students
  in the registration line . . .
    he put me
    (a total *novice*)
    in Chemistry 101-P.

The *P* indicates that you must have
  a prerequisite
  seventeen years
  of high school chemistry
  to qualify for the course!

I therefore remember little—
  here listed is most of that:
      (1) what the periodic chart is
      (2) how to spell *chart*
      (3) labs have breakage fees
      (4) melted glass is hot
      (5) the chemical expression
          for water

To my bewilderment
  we were into atoms
  on the third day
    like everyone
    was supposed to know
    what
    was
    up.

The course was *down* for me
  from
  that
  day
  on
  and on
  and on
  and on . . .

I mined this nugget, though,
  from that
  dark hole
  in my academic voyage:
    "No one
    has ever seen
    an atom."

Men have dedicated their lives
  to explaining
  something
  no one has ever seen.

The plain fact is
  all we know
  about the atom
  we know
    from what
    it does.

Oh, brother, can you feel
  the insight percolate
  the truth effervesce
  the wisdom ooze
    in
    that
    "plain fact"?

Our knowledge of God
  is like that . . .
    we know him
    not because we have seen him
    but because of what he does
      of what he is.

Certain atoms get together
  in a certain way
  and we call them
  water.

Love
Truth
Joy
Affirmation
Peace
Long-suffering
Patience
  get together
  in a certain way
  and we call them
  Jesus Christ.

The truth of God hinges on one verse
  from the Bible
  for me:
    "The word of God
    became a human being
    and walked among us"
      (John 1:14).

We saw Peter
  and in Christ
  God was *patient*.

We saw Lazarus
   and in Christ
   God was *friend*.

We saw blind Bartimaeus
   and in Christ
   God was *compassion*.
We saw parables
   and in Christ
   God was *truth*.
We saw Jesus
   and discovered God!

The theological word is *incarnation*—
   God in human flesh ...
   the mind-boggler
      that makes the atom
      as understandable
      as a kindergarten sandpile!

I, therefore, translate John 1:14
   (directly from the Aramaic)
   thus:
      "The word of God
      became a human being
      and strolled
      amongst us ..."

The hymn has it ...
   "What a friend
   we have in Jesus ..."

Hence, my word-of-the-month ...
   God in human flesh—"incarnation."
   God in Jesus Christ—"friend."
   Friendcarnation ...

FRIENDCARNATION . . .

    Like the Hallmark-card-sender
      in Jesus
      God cared enough
      to send his
      very best . . .

FRIENDCARNATION . . .

    Being called
    out of your
    Zacchaeus tree
      from your
      three-day tomb
    from your Mary-Martha
    pots and pans
      from your
      loneliness
      insecurity
      solitude
      labor
      studies
      hatred
      closed-mindedness
    into
    the
    light.

FRIENDCARNATION . . .

    To learn the meaning
    of a new word
    invented by my friend,
    Rowan Claypool . . .
        "Peacegiver."

FRIENDCARNATION . . .

In the spirit of Christ
living among
folks he considered vital . . .
    knowing without a doubt
        with gratitude
    "God
    don't
    make
    no
    junk!"

FRIENDCARNATION . . .

Hearing,
    "I will lift up my eyes
    to the hills . . .
    from whence (where)
    comes my help."
Answering,
    "Here I am!"

FRIENDCARNATION . . .

Being the gospel
according to James Taylor
        and Carole King:
    "Just call out my name
    And you know wherever I am
    I'll come running . . ."

FRIENDCARNATION . . .

Discovering God in friends . . .
Being ministered to . . .
Being found in the ditch . . .
Being lifted up . . .
Being important . . .

FRIENDCARNATION . . .

Being a slide show
  of the Holy Land
  for a man
  who'll never go . . .
Describing *blue* to a blind man
  until he knows why
  it isn't purple . . .
Sending . . .
Going . . .
Loving . . .
Hurting . . .
    like God does.

FRIENDCARNATION . . .

I'd rather flunk chemistry
  than life . . .
I'd rather do peace
  than war . . .
I'd rather be a hunk of truth
  than a body of knowledge . . .
I'd like to befriend . . .
I'd like to be Friend!

FRIENDCARNATION!

Celaborate

She'd have to take lessons
   to make enemies . . .
     her name is
     Martha Dawson.

She is widowed and lives alone now
   in an upstairs apartment
   in Shelbyville, Kentucky.

We used to exchange favors—
   I was her pastor
   she was my organist.

I was a seminary student
   full of wisdom
      insight
      help
      maturity.

But I needed Martha . . .
   she had been
   raising pastors
   for fifty years.

The jet set
would do well
to learn
all it can
from the
buggy brigade ...

At the time we were in
  Graefenburg, Kentucky
    (near Waddy
      Avenstoke
      Buffalo Lick
      Pigeon Fork)
    "center of
    the vicinity" ...

Martha came to be a recurring inspiration
  to this young parson ...
    I'm almost sure
    she thought up unaided
      rinky-tink
      ragtime piano
        and wouldn't
        take credit for it
        because she was
        church organist!

College graduate
  Ear musician par excellence
    Teacher
      Heritage appreciator
        The fulcrum
        on which
        Graefenburg culture
        pivoted.

Always sensitive to the moment
      and delightful wit
            example:
            Veteran's Day 1964
            Call to worship
            Martha "organizing"
            and I caught
               what she was doing!
                  She was
                  "fancying-up"
                  a World War I song
                  from the pop charts
                  "My Buddy"!
            I looked over at her
            and had to fight a grin—
               Martha looked up
               from the Baptist Hammond
               with the straightest
                  holiest
                  Baptist face
               you ever saw
                  and winked!

Martha has always loved people
   and the vice is versa . . .
      she is what I call
      a *rumor bucket*
      and not
      a *rumor conduit* . . .
         she knows more
         that nobody needs to know
         and keeps it that way . . .
            a beautiful heart
            that has become
            a disposal
            for rotten news.

I never knew a time when Martha
   wouldn't help
   in any worthy effort
   if she could just be
   propped up.

Which gets this story
   in the
      little
         end
           of
              the
                 funnel . . .

Martha wrote me a beautiful note
   recently . . .
      started out
      conveying how lonely she'd been
         how depressed she'd felt
      the past few days.

Since Clark's death
   she'd moved to town
   to be nearer stores
      family
      doctors.

Now quite alone for the first time
   in her full life
   she was having
   normal adjustment traumas.

The note went on . . .
   herein the random-style gist:

"The other day
I was feeling especially blue . . .
   all alone
   in this apartment
   and had been
   several days.
Finally got up
   midafternoon
   put on my hat and coat
   walked to a nearby
   old folks home.
Sat down in the parlor
   at the piano
   in my hat and coat
   and started playing
   every old song I knew—
      crowd gathered
      on crutches
      on walkers
      in wheelchairs.
We all sang
   till we were all worn out!
I got up and walked home
   in the dusky
      fading sunlight
   and I wasn't lonely
      depressed
      blue
   anymore!"

I'm glad God thought up pianos
   so Martha
   could do his work . . .

97

I'm glad God thought up Martha
  so I could
  do mine better!

To take the gifts he gives you
  To cultivate his kind of sensitivity
    To love those who need you
      To work the works of him who sent you
     To *celebrate* his love . . .
      To *labor* with his joy . . .
       CELABORATE!

CELABORATE!

Do unto others
  as God
  would have done
  for them . . .
    invest your despair
    in another man's joy
      bind up the broken
      lift up the fallen
      straighten the bent
      love the ugly
        the beautiful
    as God would . . .
    as God does . . .

CELABORATE!

The eagle was made to fly
  the fish to swim
  the rose to smell
  the sun to shine
  and you to love

to care
to give
to receive
to hurt
to feel
as God would . . .
as God does . . .

CELABORATE!

To go through life
like a Samaritan
hunting ditch-dwellers
like a father
waiting for the prodigal
like a shepherd
searching for the hundredth
as God would . . .
as God does . . .

CELABORATE!

Finding the deepest joy of discipleship
to be
not just a head full
but a heart full
and a hand full
of real compassion . . .
God-style!

CELABORATE!

With Joseph in alien circumstance
doing the work of God
With Isaiah in commitment
"Here am I; use me!"

With Peter in enthusiasm
   "I will follow . . ."
With Paul in discipline
   "This one thing I do"
With Albert Schweitzer in selflessness
   junglehugging
With Dietrich Bonhoeffer in prison
   paying for discipleship

CELABORATE!

Doing the work of God
   not because you *have* to
   but because you *want* to!
      and hearing
      "This, too, is my son
      in whom I am
      quite pleased!"

CELABORATE!

To take everything you know of yourself
   and give it
   to everything you know of God
   with all your heart
   with all your joy
      just
      for
      the
      heaven
      of
      it!

CELABORATE!

   as God would . . .
   as God does . . .

Humortality

My last two years in college were spent
    getting ready
    and
    being impatient
        to marry
        Eleanor Wilson
        Memphis, Tennessee
        Baylor, '59.

We had much fun those years
    and prided ourselves
    on a remarkable record:
        we met
            dated
            were engaged
            married
            never having had
            an argument
            in two years of relating.

Marriage counseling later showed
    the reason
    for our constant
    harmony—
          we
          both
          loved
          me!

Our first argument ever
    came after three months
    of marriage
        and scared us
        both
        to death.

I was employed on a church staff
    in Texas . . .
        the staff
        was planning
        its annual
        August picnic.
"Who will bring sandwiches?"
"Who will bring homemade ice cream?"
"Who will bring cherry pie?"
    I volunteered
    Eleanor
    for cherry pie.
    Eleanor had never made
        cherry pie . . .
        I didn't know that!

"You're going to make a cherry pie
    for the
    staff picnic."
        "I'm *what*?"

Later, she agreed to try
          pie.

Day of the picnic.
     I came home
     for lunch
     as pie was in progress . . .
          the top crust
          wouldn't do
          what top crust
          must do
          on cherry pie.

It was a woven, latticework top
     with half-inch, foot-long
     crust strips
          laced together
          like a furnace grate . . .
               but hers
               was in trouble
               because the pie
               was cherry-poor
                    one cherry deep
                    a cherry here
                    a cherry there
               the crust
               dipped down
               between cherries!

I tried to help
     I teased a little . . .
          I didn't realize
          Eleanor's
          professional cooking
          reputation
          was at stake
          in the annual

August
church staff
"eatouttogether."

At the picnic I teased further . . .
"Don't-try-that-pie-you'll-die!"
We all laughed.
Except Eleanor.
She could only
smile
tight-toothed
thin-lipped.

Our first argument ever
lasted all evening.

I'd thought it funny
hilarious
teasing
humorous
she'd found it painful
insensitive
unbearable.

A contrast, if you please . . .
in the fifty-years-married
marriage of
Kyle and Erma Milton.

Erma was the patron saint
of Kentucky
country cookers.

Kyle was a farmer/deacon
in the church I served
as pastor
while in seminary.

They had our family of four over
>   for dinner
>   one night . . .
>   four meats
>   chicken
>   ribs
>   pork chops
>   steak
>   cooked out on the grill
>   twelve fresh vegetables
>   several relishes
>   homemade rolls
>   pre-sweetened tea
>   two cakes
>   a pie.

As we arrived at the house
>   Kyle was coming in
>   from the field
>   and saw the meat
>   smoking too much
>   on the grill—
>   "Erma!
>   Meat's burnin'!"

Erma roared out with sweat and anguish
>   on her face
>   flipped meat
>   like army pancakes
>   and partially
>   rescued dinner.

She was embarrassed . . .
>   pastor and family over
>   wanted to do her best
>   burned the meat . . .

Kyle pulled an "early-married-Grady"
    "Pass some more
        of that burnt meat . . ."
    "Grady, get some more
        of that burnt meat . . ."
    "Boys, how 'bout some more
        of that burnt meat . . ."

Erma didn't even tight-tooth
            thin-lip a grin . . .
    she smouldered
        glared
        fumed.

One pork chop remained on the platter . . .
    Kyle offered it to me
            to Eleanor
            to the boys . . . .
    finally he said to Erma:
        "Well, pass me
        that last piece
        of burnt meat . . ."

Erma finally let it fly!
    Well, *Kylemilton*—
        you sure ate
        enough of that
        burnt meat . . ."

Kyle looked up at the maddest face
    I've seen
    in years . . .
        we all froze
        Eleanor
        the boys
        and I all stopped
        in mid-chew

and stared at one
                    then
                    the other.

Much marriage had taught Kyle
            about Erma . . .
                    he knew
                    he was in trouble
                    and deserved it . . .
            then humor saved the day
                    his eyes twinkled
                    a grin started
                    a fifty-year marriage
                    was about to prove
                    its mettle . . .

"Well, Erma, if you hadn't burnt it
            there just wouldn't
            have been enough!"

She laughed till she cried.
We laughed with her.
Kyle ate his burnt pork chop
            with a twinkle
            and a grin.

He'd been rough on her
            and was sorry;
She'd been too uptight about supper
            and knew it.

I sat there wishing I'd known how
            to humor cherry pie
            like Kyle could
                    humor burnt meat!

And such is the way of the man
    who learns to live
    with humor . . .
        it is his
        touch with life.

I call it *humortality*—
    to live life
    with humor.

HUMORTALITY

To live with sensitivity
        with fun
        with joy
        with affirmation . . .
    to smile
        at dipping-crust
        cherry pie
        and burnt meat
        and know
        this too shall pass!

HUMORTALITY

A bandage for the open-sored
    self-consciousness
    of life—
        when what you *do*
        is how you think
        people discover
            what you *are*.

HUMORTALITY

Overcoming enough pain
                    embarassment
                    stupidity
   to begin to say
      "I did that dumb thing
      before and lived!"

HUMORTALITY

The ability to laugh
   at a hammer-hit thumb
   after the nail
   has grown back!

HUMORTALITY

Not *avoiding* conflict
but *enduring* conflict . . .
   knowing that
      God goes with you
      through the valley
      of the shadow of death
        not *around* it!

HUMORTALITY

Experiencing enough of life
   to see disaster
   in perspective . . .
      slaves singing spirituals
      instead of
      committing suicide . . .
        a blind man
        saying: "Good
        to see you"
           and then
           chuckling . . .

joking about the
cast on your leg
at the ski lodge!

HUMORTALITY

Knowing at last that
 a temporary setback
 is not a permanent handicap
  and
  a permanent handicap
  can be a temporary
  setback.

HUMORTALITY

Burnt meat teaching cherry pie
 sensitivity
 fun
 wit
  can turn a disaster
  into a love feast!

HUMORTALITY!

Togetherapy

One of the happiest years of my life
>   was my
>   freshman year
>   in college . . .
>>   I was at
>>   Wayland College
>>   Plainview, Texas.

The year was a mosiac
>   of friends
>>   experiences
>>   maturing
>>   learning
>>   frolicking
>>   failing typing
>>   being away from home.

My greatest delight that year
>   was my participation
>   in the Wayland
>>   International Choir—
>>>   forty-two voices
>>>   costumes
>>>   good music
>>>   traveling.

111

We sang in seventeen foreign languages
    plus
    English
    with
    a
    Texas accent!

As part of my musical experience
    I sang
    in a quartet
    with Ed Clark
        Jim Hart
        Elmore Averyt
    called "The Troubadors."

It was—in the words of Sinatra—
    "a
    very
    good
    year . . ."
        a year
        of impressions
        I will
        never forget
            and will
            work
            to remember.

Amidst the glow of that year
    was a tragedy
    from which
    I learned
    one of my
    first and deepest
    theological truths:
        a truth about
            life and death
            tragedy and joy—

The spring of 1953 marks
  the death
  of one of God's
  best friends . . .
    Dr. Lake Pylant . . .
      Old Testament teacher
      friend of students
      jovial citizen
      husband of Agnes
      father of Patsy.

Lake Pylant died in the crash
  of a small
    private plane . . .
  flying was in
  the family blood
    Patsy was a pilot
    by the time
    she could drive
    a stick-shift Ford
  (we called Patsy Pylant
     "Patsy Pilot") . . .

The death of Lake Pylant
  hit our small
    500-member
    campus
  like a thunderbolt.

If the students had voted
  he'd have had
  the first full page
  in *every* annual!
    a real
    favorite . . .
      an unbelievable
      loss.

I attended the funeral
    and cried
    all the way through
        along with
        an entire
        College Avenue
        Baptist Churchful.

The congregation filed outside
        stood on the lawn
        waited to view
            the casket
            being pallborne
            to the funeral cars.

And there in that group
    I saw a sight
    I will never
        be able
        to erase
        from my memory's eye ...
            it is chiseled
            in the granite
            of my past:
                As the casket
                came down the steps
                in the loving hands
                of devoted friends
                    Agnes
                    and
                    "Patsy Pilot"
                    followed it
                        smiling!

None who knew them
         could have ever imagined it
         as a "smile-for-the-church"
         or a "witness-in-your-grief"
         sort of thing—
                 a whimpering
                 "grin-of-the-soul"
                 that said with
                 bland shallowness:
                         "God must
                         have needed/wanted
                         him more
                         than we did!"

The thought would be blasphemy!
         rather than a bland
                             pious
                             grin-no-matter-what
         the radiant faith
         of Agnes and Patsy
                 spoke to me
                 then as now
                 of a faith in God
                 that is not sidetracked
                 by momentary disaster.

Several years ago
         a lady in Florida
         stormed into the study
         of her minister
         to "dump" on him
         because her house
         had been flattened
         by a hurricane ...

in her words
"she prayed and prayed
that God would spare
her house . . ."
"What kind of God
would let that happen . . ."
and the minister
took his licks.

Finally, the minister stood
looked the lady
right in the eye
and said:
"Maybe
he was busy
with his regular
customers!"

Agnes and Patsy Pylant were
his
regular
customers . . .

I have followed Agnes with loving concern
through the years . . .
she is one
of the most radiant
human beings
I have ever known;
my contacts with Patsy
have been less frequent
but have proven
to have depth
beyond imagination . . .

the point is this—
        they both epitomize
        today's great word
        from the young set:
        TOGETHERNESS.

They radiate joy
They love freely
They believe in God
        more deeply than
        some families
        that still have husbands/fathers ...
                they bring some strong
                Apart
                        to life's *Shattered*
                        and practice *Together.*

Groups need Togetherness
Individuals need Togetherness
There is rich benefit in its therapy ...
        hence, the word-of-the-month:
                TOGETHERAPY ...
                        linking your *apart*
                        to your brother's *alone*
                        meeting needs jointly ...
                the therapy of together ...
                TOGETHERAPY!

TOGETHERAPY!

Heed the word of Apostle Bacharach:
        "What the world needs now
        Is love, sweet love ..."
Balming the wounds of life
because you care ...

TOGETHERAPY!

Dedicating your life
to the belief
that the "One Note Samba"
    cannot carry the luggage
    of a Beethoven Symphony ...

TOGETHERAPY!

The glue
that mortars
desperate voyagers
to one another
    sufficiently
    strong enough
        to escape
        the *Poseidon* ...
while realizing
that *together*
is a better basis
for travel
    than
    for escape ...

TOGETHERAPY!

The face-saving
    live-saving discovery
        that you are not
        the *first*
        to have this dilemma
          and that others
          have survived ...

TOGETHERAPY!

Weaving the threads
of circumstance
 into a tapestry
 of purpose . . .
  knitting the strands
  of consequence
  so tightly around purpose
   that you couldn't
   pull a runner
   with a longshoreman's hook!

TOGETHERAPY!

The ability
to need another . . .
 the ability
 to support another . . .
  the ability
  to love another . . .
   the ability
   to be loved
   by another . . .

The feeling of healing
The taste of joy
The comfort of being
 God's regular customer . . .

TOGETHERAPY!

Not just *survival*
 but *living!*
Get it together . . .
then
Get it *together!*

TOGETHERAPY!

Matrimonotony

It is a strange pull
　　like the moon
　　on the tide
　　　　that monthly
　　　　　　pulls me
　　to the theme
　　of *The Student*
　　　　with an insight
　　　　that hopefully
　　　　will interpret
　　　　that theme ...

For six weeks I thought *this* month
　　would be
　　the exception ...
　　　　thanks to George Kovacs
　　　　I have my idea!
　　　　　　Thanks,
　　　　　　George ...

George Kovacs is the owner
    of a contemporary
        lighting device
        store in New York City
        and regularly
        buys space
        to advertise his
                contemporary
                lighting
                devices
                    in the
                    New Yorker
                    magazine . . .

The October 15, 1973, *New Yorker*
    has an ad
    on page 60
    that could make George Kovacs
    a millionaire
    by
    October 18, 1973 . . .
        it begins:
            "Save your marriage
            for $39.50 . . ."
        it concludes:
            "Just add $2.50
            for shipping . . ."

George claims—tongue in cheek—
    to be able
        for $39.50
        plus $2.50 for shipping
    to save your marriage
    with a contemporary
        lighting
        device . . .

What a missionary to matrimony!
    Anywhere in the world
    George can shed light
    on your marital darkness
        for $39.50
        plus $2.50 for shipping!

He just must be elated!
    a chipper
        shipper to the harried
                married!

He is surely—*most surely*—not serious
    but some soul out there
    who married a catastrophe
    will make out a check
    for $42.00
        and await the arrival—
           postpaid—
        of connubial bliss . . .

Too many marriages are in trouble
    because couples
    try to patch them up
    with gadgets—
        simple solutions
        to
        complex problems.

I have been happily married
    for eleven years

        and unhappily married
        for five years
        before that . . .

                    all
                    to
                    the
                    same
                    woman—
                        Eleanor!

Emotionally and actually we bought
        every gadget
        that promised
        unity
            harmony
                bliss
                    peace
                        togetherness
                            and
                            were
                            miserable!

The main problem we had—to quote Eleanor—
        was
        that we couldn't agree
        on who
            loved
            me
            most!

She was my reflection
            my possession
            my support force
            my child-raiser-in-residence
                and we
                nearly
                lost
                it.

She wisely sought help
  thankfully found it . . .
  the restoration process began
  and has continued.

What we discovered finally
  was what Kahlil Gibran
  describes beautifully
  in *The Prophet:*
    to paraphrase
    he says that
    marriage is *not*
    two islands
    becoming one land mass . . .
      it is rather
      two islands
      remaining distinct
        whose shores
        are washed
        by the
        mutual waters
        of love!

(Here imagine a background accompaniment
  bursting forth
  with tympani
  of *The Hallelujah Chorus!*)

The light we finally saw more clearly
  came to us
  in the form
  of a basic truth:
    when she is she
    and
    when I am I
      we please each other most!

Two people living only to please each other
           to limit each other
              to bargain with each other
              to endure each other
        are living what I call

              MATRIMONOTONY ...
                    the deadly art
                    of living together
                    without
                    loving together ...
              a relationship
              that is what my friend
                    Herb Barks
              calls:
                    "a rut, not a groove ..."

Eleanor and I have tried to learn
        from Tarzan and Jane ...
              you will swing best
              and go farthest
              on the strong vines
                    and you must
                    turn loose of one
                    to grab the next ...
                          hence, progress
                          change
                          learning
                          growth
                          joy
                          togetherness.
Avoid matrimonotony ...
        don't patch up with gadgets
        build with solid *stuff*
              don't demand
              learn to give

　　　　　don't fear
　　　　　learn to swing free . . .

MATRIMONOTONY
　　　the absolute boredom
　　　of "we-can-afford-em"
　　　　　mistaking happiness
　　　　　　　for accumulating
　　　　　　　for agreeing
　　　　　　　for unruffled waters
　　　　　　　for peace-at-any-price . . .

MATRIMONOTONY
　　　having your rich oak
　　　"termited"
　　　　　by taking each other for granted
　　　　　by demanding "do-it-my-way"
　　　　　by self-centeredness
　　　　　by forgetting to say:
　　　　　　　"You're beautiful/handsome"
　　　　　　　"Thanks for helping with dishes"
　　　　　　　"Let me keep the children
　　　　　　　　　while you go
　　　　　　　　　out to lunch
　　　　　　　　　with Suzy . . ."
　　　　　　　"I love you . . ."

MATRIMONOTONY
　　　believing "the family that prays together
　　　　　　　　stays together"
　　　but never agreeing on anything
　　　　　except that *we will pray together!*"
　　　　　　　and believing that
　　　　　　　　　staying together
　　　　　　　　　regardless
　　　　　　　　　has merit of its own . . .

MATRIMONOTONY
    willingness to stay the same
    rather than experiment
       grow
       try new things
       re-evaluate constantly
    missing the joy
    of new places to eat
      new friends to eat with
      new arenas of freedom
         with each other
         with others
      new horizons to explore . . .

MATRIMONOTONY
    dreading time alone ("What will we say?"
                   "What will we do?"
                   "I'm tired of TV!")
    failing to be inventive with autumn walks
             Saturday brunch
             hamburgers at midnight

MATRIMONOTONY
    becoming so much parent to children
    that you forget to be lover
             husband/wife
             celebrator of love/life
             cute/handsome . . .

MATRIMONOTONY
    the tragedy of missing what could have been
    because you failed *together*
        to work
        at what could only be done
          together!

MATRIMONOTONY
two islands becoming one land mass
two candles being blown out
   so one can burn alone
two lives dying so one can live
two minus signs trying to multiply
   and produce a positive . . .
      and being
      divided
      in the process . . .

ATTENTION GEORGE KOVACS . . .
you won't sell
a contemporary
   lighting
   device
at the Nutt-house . . .
     your price is
     too low . . .
       and therefore
       way
       too
       high!

Carepooling

I am sitting at my business desk . . .
    the drop-down tray
    of a DC-9 jet
        dropped-down . . .
                notebook out
                pencil flying . . .

I have just come from the University of Florida
    and an attend-workout
        out-for-dinner
        spend-the-night
        hate-to-part
    visit with one of God's choice men . . .
        John C-for-Calvin Lotz
        and wife Vicki . . .

John is head basketball coach
    for the Florida
        Fightin' (always clean!)
        Gators . . .

We were classmates in college at Baylor University . . .
　　we had to mature
　　to come to know
　　　　love each other . . .
　　　　(and we really do!)
　　the reason was
　　　　John was an athlete
　　　　I was a campus-christian
　　　　who prayed for athletes
　　　　　　but never
　　　　　　spoke to them!

I would not trade college for my current friendship
　　with John and Vicki . . .
　　I am the current non-resident
　　　　　　Florida
　　　　　　Fightin' (always clean!)
　　　　　　Gators
　　　　　　Booster Band
　　　　　　Tip-Off Club
　　　　　　support force!

John has burned to coach basketball
　　like Paul burned
　　to evangelize Gentiles . . .
　　　　in fact,
　　　　if John had been Paul
　　　　Damascus could beat UCLA
　　　　today . . .

He coached four years in high school
　　then became assistant coach
　　　　　　chief recruiter
　　　　　　shooting wizard

at the University of North Carolina
for eight years ...
under Dean Smith (head coach)
and John Lotz (see above)
the Tarheels of NC
were the second team
in all the US
behind John Wooden's
UCLA trophy-hogs ...

In April, 1973, John C-for-Calvin Lotz
became head basketball coach
at the University of Florida ...
injuries
misfortune
demons
genetics
have all conferred
have all decided
he shall not have
an easy first year ...
John stuck out his tongue
raspberried injuries
misfortune
demons
genetics
declaring:
"Help!"

His tallest man (well enough to walk) is
six-feet-five-inches tall ...
sports writers
have dubbed the Gators
"Lotz' Leprechauns!"
John loves it!

The players love him . . .
    he has them in his home
    he counsels on dating
                religion
                wardrobe
                vocation
                and how hard you have to work
                to be part
                of this committed crew . . .

In a recent interview for a newspaper
    a starter on his team
    talking about Lotz
    said:
        "Coach Truax is *Mister Offense* . . .
        Coach Grubar is *Mister Defense* . . .
        Coach Lotz is *Mister Everything!*"

I have not met three preachers in ten years
    who read more theology
                sermons
                ethics
                etc.
    than John C-for-Calvin Lotz . . .

He is easily one of the two or three
    most unselfish
        compassionate
        faithful friends I know . . .

He is seeking to instill in his players
    and fellow coaches
    a sense of desire
        discipline
        will-to-win
        fight (always clean!)
        compassion

that teaches basketball players
what churches need to learn:
"there's no competition
between lighthouses!"
he's eager for you to thrill
because you assisted
passed off
set a teammate up
as much as if you had scored . . .
he's concerned that players
burn the varnish off the court
wear the dimples off the
bottoms of Converse shoes . . .
run
run
run
(imagine 300 more "runs")
and run until any team
that plays the Gators
will feel they've
just parked their iceberg
in a boiling ocean!

As I write these words John is in transit
with his team
to Houston, Texas,
where David will meet Goliath tomorrow
at the University of Houston . . .
tonight at 10:00 P.M.
John C-for-Calvin Lotz
will begin what will be a tradition . . .
he will go to each room
sit with each player
leave a brief paper/book/thought
and say in his own way:

"I believe in you . . .
I'm proud of you . . .
Thanks for letting me
be your coach . . ."

Tonight each player will read the first such paper:
Lotz wrote a paper
entitled "Mental Conditioning"
with five points . . .
fifth point is entitled
Religion . . .
in it he shares his faith
as a Christian
and encourages each player
to be aware of his need for God
in his daily life . . .

He's off to a super start . . .
His players are unusually fortunate . . .
God is undoubtedly pleased . . .
The Southeastern Conference
is in
for trouble . . .

I have two sons who are super kids
super athletes . . .
I'd give my right arm
up to the left shoulder
to have a Lotz-like coach
coach them in life
in basketball
in faith . . .

In fact I wish I were nineteen
talented
and on his team . . .

Here is what the church is about, to me . . .
businessmen
teachers
farmers
merchants
all adding their point five
to daily life.

I should learn to care for my partners
my family
my friends
my world
in a John C-for-*Care* Lotz kind of way . . .
excelling in my vocation
driving hard (always clean!)
giving unashamedly
caring with all my heart . . .

To pool this kind of care and compassion
would turn the church
into a John C-for-Care *Lotz* better place . . .
pooling our care . . .
a "carepool . . ."

CAREPOOLING

To rip up a roof
so you can
let down a friend
to the only help
that matters
in the long run . . .

CAREPOOLING

A team spirit that delights
    when no one cares
    who gets credit for success
        victory
        accomplishment . . .
    Baptists being glad
    when Methodists reach more folks
    than ever before . . .
        "limited water"
        but unlimited love . . .

CAREPOOLING

Making the church an
    unselfish
    compassionate
    concerned
    band of Samaritans
        in search of
        ditchdwellers . . .

CAREPOOLING

Thirstquenching
Hungersatisfying
Nakedclothing
Prisonervisiting
    because we love
    not
    because we get credit . . .

CAREPOOLING

To *be* a cooperative program
Not just vote for it . . .

CAREPOOLING
Serving and ministering
to a community
campus
nation
whether anyone joins
our group
or not ...

CAREPOOLING

Treating God's world
God's way ...
like a coach
not
like a referee ...
remembering:
"God sent his Son
into the world
not to condemn the world
but that through him
the world
might be saved ..."

CAREPOOLING ...

Caring enough
to give our very best ...
together!